My Past Way

of

Budo

And Other Essays

Including an essay by
Katsaharu K. Nakazono

Mikoto Masahilo Nakazono

My Past Way of Budo

Published by Kototama Books

ISBN 13: 978-0-9716674-0-2
ISBN 10: 0-9716674-0-3

The essay, My Past Way of Budo, originally edited by Nikos Colias, 1972

Cover design: Brian Brigham

First printing   1979 Piñon Fast Print
Second printing 1990 Piñon Fast Print
Third Printing   2002 Piñon Fast Print
Fourth printing 2006 Piñon Fast Print

This book was printed on 100% pcw recycled paper.

Shrine at The Kototama Institute, Santa Fe, New Mexico
(1978 - 1985).

TABLE OF CONTENTS

My Past Way of Budo

Part One

I began my studies by practicing Kendo at the age of six with my uncle. At twelve I started Judo practice and, at about nineteen, I began Karate. I studied the lance and many other forms of Budo* and finally Aikido, which I studied with O Sensei Ueshiba, who is now deceased. When I met O Sensei, I believed his was the highest form of Budo.

Since childhood, I had heard the words "Budo spirit" a thousand, million times over and I tried to discover what this meant, asking all of my teachers about it. No one could give me a satisfactory answer. The response was usually, "Don't talk about it - practice! Your exercise will give you the answer." Another response, a reprimand, would be, "Each time before practice, decide to die. There's no need to ask such a question." I tried to follow these instructions, but no answer came to my inner questions. I then studied all kinds of books on Budo that were written in ancient times. I finally got a rough answer; the meaning of Budo is to die. That is why,

1

although I often had broken or dislocated bones or would lose consciousness during a competition, my physical pain or difficulties never stopped or discouraged me. Pain was an ever present reality despite my inner resolve.

At the initial shock of a bone breaking or a bullet penetrating the body, there is no feeling of pain. The mind unconsciously concentrates, but afterwards, when the mind returns to normal, the pain is terrible. I had such experiences many times and, in the beginning, I felt that pain or suffering could be overcome by mental control. This kind of transcendence I thought equivalent to what Zen and Budo teachings call the void state. My new perception of Budo was that its purpose was the continued extension of the transcending mind. With this new outlook, others automatically began to call me "teacher". I was obliged to explain to them what I had studied and experienced; younger people very happily studied and practiced with me. However, somewhere deep inside there remained a dark hole or void and as I got older its size increased.

My Budo practice, the meaningless experiences of the war, leaving me with a kind of criminal sense, and feeling this dark void, all culminated in my becoming a perfect nihilist. This was happening around the time when World War II was coming to a close; I was twenty-nine years old and in the middle of the Indonesian jungles. The nihilism I was experiencing was antagonistic to my physical life and to society as well.

Although I was totally disinterested in actual life, the inner desire to fill this hole was ever present. It led me to the Shugendo teacher, Sakai Sensei. Shugendo was originally an ancient Shinto exercise to grasp the Kototama Principle. It was later changed into a Buddhist system after the principle was hidden. Many Japanese today believe they are a religious sect. Sakai Sensei addresses Jizo Bosatsu as a symbolic god; a very special symbol, not a god of Shinto or a Buddha. All other named gods or Buddhas are carefully kept in shrines, but this one is different. Statues of Jizo Bosatsu are placed throughout Japan along the roadways and they are as playmates to passing children. When I first met Sakai Sensei he immediately said to me, before I had opened my mouth, "Your ancestors' souls are not quiet, they have no base. If you have a statue of Jizo Bosatsu, this will be their place and they will become quiet. Then your future health and fortune will improve." I asked, "What is Jizo Bosatsu?" He answered, "It is a stone statue which symbolizes all souls which have manifested into the finite world and have now returned to the infinite world. This includes humans, plants, stones, etc., anything which once existed in the limited world. Some happily returned to the infinite but some wished to remain behind, still attached to the finite world. It is for those who remain behind that this statue can offer a space to stay happily in the finite world." This explanation satisfied me. At that time, my body was completely spoiled from the three years spent in the Indonesian jungles and, as I said, my spiritual condition was similar. Like a drowning man who will grasp at anything, I acquired a statue of Jizo Bosatsu as Sakai Sensei had suggested.

At this time, I was studying with Ueshiba Sensei to learn the spiritual base or source from which he had created Aikido. I was also studying the diet principles of Ohsawa Sensei, the founder of macrobiotics. All of these studies

3

and practices greatly added to my growth, yet still my inner void or hole was not filled. My suffering continued as I questioned the reason for it. To society, I was considered a teacher, but inside the lack of complete confidence created a terribly heavy life. Other teachers seemed perfectly content and concentrated on their work and I wondered about their abilities. I continued this difficult life until I finally came to Ogasawara Sensei's Kototama Principle. My age was approaching fifty.

Looking back, the first fifty years of my life were like a spiritual odyssey which had finally brought me to the country of the Bluebird*. With my understanding of the Kototama, my view of life turned around 180 degrees. What I had grasped up to this time, that which had seemed so meaningful to me, I now saw as very small and insignificant. I saw that what I valued was also the cause of my confusion because I was operating in a world that was only relative. From that moment, my Budo underwent great changes. The practice of overcoming physical and spiritual obstacles changed to one of acceptance towards all kinds of difficulties.

This is no easier than the other way; in fact, it is a much more difficult practice. To accept, one must stand outside of this finite world or there can be no acceptance of it. With the Kototama as a mirror, one can see where spiritual and physical difficulties are being created. Why would one wish to conquer these difficulties? The relationship of one's lower dimensions to a "fighting" mind can be seen at those times. If the origin of difficulties and the source of this "fighting" mind can be seen, and we can accept these things as natural, then we can stand away from them with a perfectly peaceful mind.

When bones break, there is physical pain; when a brother or sister dies, there is profound grief. To try to forget this pain or sadness with a fighting mind, regardless of how much power such a method creates, ultimately cheats our self. This practice becomes habitual and we dig our private hells with it. Because we live in it, we cannot see our own everyday hell world.

There is only one absolute a priori life-will of beings, **I**, which creates the human body and invests it with physical power, **WI** . Ueshiba O Sensei tried to explain this with the words "Ki" and "Ko-Kyu", but I could not clearly grasp this from his explanation. I remember that he, too, was not fully clear about this because he followed the Ohmoto Shinto sect. Between the a priori human life-will, **I**, and the human body's power, **WI**, there are eight motive powers or vibrations. These he grasped instinctively and wanted to manifest them through Budo movement, thus founding Aikido. However, the Ohmoto sect, as with all other Shinto sects, does not purely transmit the Kototama Principle. That is why he could not exactly explain with words what he could grasp in a priori.

In reference to "Ki" and "Ko-Kyu", "Ki" is already within **WI** and then expands with movement as "Ko-Kyu", but "Ki" and "Ko-Kyu" imply a manifestation of physical power. This is not a clear explanation of **I** and **WI** from the viewpoint of the Kototama Principle. On this point, O Sensei, himself, had some inner confusion. It is at this point that all spiritual and religious seekers finally have difficulty. They can grasp it but without the Kototama Principle they have no way of transmitting it to others.

5

When someone attracts a following by giving a symbolic explanation of what he, himself, has grasped in a priori, spirit or soul world, and is satisfied with such a state of affairs, this seeker is as yet a beginner. The one who is at the end of his grasping of a priori and still suffers because he's not able to hand it over to others is the real seeker.

As one seriously searches the self and begins to know about it, there develops a deep sense of insecurity, a terrible kind of void feeling which creates fear. Fear automatically gives rise to an attitude of guarded attention, a fighting mind that needs to control. Many leaders in society resort to tricky words and techniques in order to captivate people with their charisma while they dig a deeper and larger hole within themselves. The Budo practicant has this same kind of fear in the very depths of himself as he develops his expertise. He needs his own satisfaction as well as corroboration from others. From my past experience, to improve physical strength and Budo techniques, one must fight to conquer one's physical and spiritual obstacles. However, no matter how far we progress, we can never find a perfect solution for ourself. Physical power and technical intelligence improve but if we seriously watch our inner activity, if we wish to be faithful to ourself, we see the hole getting bigger in proportion to that improvement. It's alright if at this point we can reconcile ourselves to it but I absolutely could not accept it. I couldn't use such cheating words as "that's life!" Hardest of all, there was no place to run.

1. Budo: Bu - physical movement; Do - Tao, Logos. The true way of physical action exactly follows the activity of a proiri Life Will. This definition was later narrowed to apply only to the martial arts of the Samurai period of Japan. The goal of their exercise was to open up to their highest human capacity. Today, people misunderstand this to mean self-defense or a sportive activity.

2. Coming from Scandinavian mythology.

Part Two

Since childhood, I had excellent Budo teachers. They all explained that competitive practice, fighting or winning in relation to another, was the wrong way, and that the object was to conquer one's own weak or negative mind. That's why I never practiced with the idea of self-defense. Self-defense doesn't exist if we refuse to fight with others. That is its real meaning. It sounds better to say "self-defense" instead of "fighting" but it's the same thing. Getting over the fighting mind is what Budo is all about. To do this, we must cleanse our mind of all its negative aspects in order to allow the morality and judgment of a clean mirror. This is the true way of Budo exercise. The state of having a clean mirror is called mei-kyou and means to grasp the mirror of life; Yata or Iota. It's a mind that is tranquil, undisturbed by a wave or ripple, so that all phenomena are reflected with perfect clarity and can be judged accordingly.

The final objective of Budo exercise is to cultivate the highest human capacity. If we hate someone, our mind is immediately unbalanced; if we have fear, our mind becomes turbulent. Joy and sadness also create imbalance in the mind and spirit for the Budo practicant. If we're sick, mei-kyou cannot exist. Any kind of aggressive or defensive desire causes disharmony and disturbs the mind. To thoroughly explore the very source of this, we must stand outside of the physical senses, which means "to die". If we decide to die, that resolution in itself is a hindrance and causes an imbalance. The only way is to get into the absolute void, the sense of nothing.

The original meaning of the competitive system in Budo was to test and clarify one's state of mind by seeing it manifest in one's actual capacity. Today no one talks or teaches this way; competition is a test for a grade or prize. O Sensei knew this and didn't allow any competition in Aikido practice. This was beautiful, yet the grading system remained to later become a cancer, guiding the Aikido student opposite to O Sensei's wishes. With serious exercise, we can unconsciously enter the void state but it's difficult to remain there and easy to fall back to our usual mindset again, thus losing mei-kyou.

If, with our ordinary viewpoint, we reflect upon the kind of power and judgment that emerges from the void state, we can see how impossible it is to repeat such exceptional actions, no matter how hard we try. One wonders how and what kind of superior power arises through our body, but traditional Budo has no answer. We can be certain, due to many repeated experiences, that superior powers do manifest through the body from a state of void or muga. One simply enjoys the muga state and the experience of various powers, or like myself, tries to realize the source; the how and why of these powers. I may be the only one who questions this way. My teachers

10

said Budo means to enter muga, to die, but I could not leave it at that. That's why my way became so hard.

I could see from my experience what wonderful powers manifest from a state of muga but I wanted to see inside this world. It was this incompleteness that was creating the ever-growing inner hole inside of me. Muga experiences do not only occur through Budo exercise. There is the example of a deathbed patient who, when his house caught fire, picked up his bed and carried it outside with him. A seventy year old woman, when confronted with her grandson being pinned down by an automobile, was able to lift the car from the child's body. There is an ancient Chinese story which says that a man meeting a tiger at midnight shoots it with his bow. Afterwards, he sees it was no tiger at all, but a large rock. Nevertheless, the arrow had been sent with such force that it had deeply pierced the rock. Many such stories exist in all parts of the world. A terminal cancer patient prays to his god and the cancer cells disappear. It is my belief that such a prayer is not an appeal for God's help, but instead he has completely given up everything, including all hope, and hands over the totality of his life into God's hands, thus entering the void state.

This prayer from a muga state can create a cure. Many scientists or doctors refuse to accept this, saying they won't believe it unless they see it with their own eyes. These people don't know the uncertainty of our physical eyes. Many easily dismiss things by saying, "It's not scientific", but the scientific "eye" means only the capacity of our physical eyes amplified by machines. This point they don't like to reflect upon.

Even after forty years of exercising and searching, I wasn't able to find the answer to how exceptional powers could manifest during Budo practice. There were none in science, religion, philosophy or any other area of knowledge in today's civilization.

It was the Kototama Principle that finally gave me a perfect answer. It is the principle of the Messiah; without it, Jesus and Buddha would have been only normal men. The esteem the world holds for them is finally directed to the principle they had within themselves. Their understanding made them who they were, so the reality of Messiah lies within that principle. It's been hidden in the dogma and symbolism of the world's philosophies, religions and mythologies. When we understand the Kototama, we can see that the words and teachings of the great saints were all expressions of this principle. They never taught it directly or explained it clearly; instead it was spoken of symbolically as manna, iota (or one jot of i), Logos, Tao, etc. They never talked about the principle itself. They only used metaphors because our ancestors had decided to hide the Kototama, as it is written in obscure, ancient Shinto documents. Moses, Lao-tzu, Jesus, Mohammed, etc., all the world's saints, absorbed exactly the same principle. Once they had grasped it, automatically they received their ancestors' hidden decision, irrespective of the fact that they lived at different times and in different places.

This may seem strange to some readers but once you have this principle of life, the Kototama, my words will seem quite reasonable. All that exists, manifest and unmanifest, is in our spirit. It exists in our being, both conscious and unconscious, in Naka-Ima (here-now). All of the past exists in our memory, which is **O** dimension, in this present life moment. Standing in **O** with **A** dimension's power to expand and imagine is how the future of all beings exists here and now. The true time and place of the existence of the past and future is Naka-Ima. I, the life-will of beings, creator of time and space, and **WI**, the physical life-power of beings, are both expanding and active in here-now. Human life-will, **I**, transforms to human physical capacity, **WI**. This gives life to the five physical senses, **U**, the memory or intellectual capacity, **O**, the emotional capacity, **A**, and the judgment and moral capacity which is **E**. **I-WI** gives power to the four dimensions and their activity gives birth to all human capacity.

We see the world from two different perspectives: **U** dimension senses the limited world, that of form, color, sound, taste, etc., creating the finite world of physical realization, and **A** dimension's capacity grasps that which is infinite. The experiences of these two "eyes", acting in here-now, are recorded in **O** dimension which then becomes knowledge. All that is grasped is put into order (time and space), separated and judged by **E** dimension. The highest morality is a consequence of **E** dimension. The life-world, that of Kototama-Futomani, can only be grasped with the "eye" of **A** dimension. It can't be grasped with **U** dimension's capacity; not seen, heard, smelled nor touched with the physical senses.

Since the Life Principle was hidden around eight thousand years ago, we have built a scientific-material civilization which is based primarily on the **U** dimension capacity. This was done purposefully by the order and guidance of our ancestors' souls and is the reason why

13

our present civilization is cut off from the world of life. Religion and philosophy are expressions of **A** dimension activity but their source, the Kototama, the principle of the Word of God and the Tao, has been hidden. Thus no one can find the origin of **A** dimension's capacity. Our spirit has been floating in the sky, moving with the clouds, not knowing where to go or what to do, like a jellyfish in the sea. In this kind of world, humanity has tried to develop and utilize to the fullest the experience and intelligence of **U** and **O** dimensions, to create and maintain the second, scientific, civilization. It was at the end of this civilization that my body was born in the south of Japan. As I've said before, I searched the spiritual world through my Budo and finally arrived at the Kototama Principle. It was a very long and difficult voyage.

"Ask, and it shall be given to you; seek, and you shall find; knock, and it shall be opened unto you. For everyone that asks, receives; and he who seeks, finds; and to him who knocks it shall be opened." (Matthew, 7:7,8). I found this teaching of Jesus and I understood that it is from my ancestors and especially for me. The ancient teachings and traditional symbols of mei-kyou (pure mirror) or muga (void) were suggestive of how to arrive at the Life Principle. After I understood this, I could overcome the karma of more than fifty years of physical life. Until then, I had felt compelled to fight with mountains, oceans, heaven, earth, society, individuals, with physical and mental suffering and to struggle with the fatigue that it brought. I could see clearly how the source of this fighting mind grew out of my undeveloped dimensions. Then I could freely accept all, good or bad. Only with the cessation of pain or difficulty can we fully accept it. In grasping the Kototama Principle, I could see with this mirror the source of these difficulties in myself and the sufferings of the past were transformed to a happiness and a kind of thankfulness.

Part Three

At the source of all fighting minds, there is love; the inner desire to return to the one source. Physical life, **WI**, is trying to synchronize with **I**, the source or spirit, and return to following the order **I-WI**. I and **WI** are two sides of the same thing, the essential substance, the human being itself, creating the activity of the four dimensions, **U**, **O**, **A**, and **E**, through physical life. When this activity is out of order, instead of harmonizing, it manifests as the fighting mind. Our capacities are completely distinct and different from one another; **U** - the five physical senses, **O** - memory or intelligence, **A** - emotion, and **E** - judgment. If we cannot stand on **I-WI**, the self, which orders these four dimensions, we aren't able to judge what we have grasped. We cannot realize what is correct.

Without grasping **I-WI**, life-will and life-power, our highest judgment, **E**, cannot be freely expressed. Without the mirror of the Life Principle, words and actions become fragmented; truth is a word instead of a reality. The current of the last eight thousand years, our present

17

scientific-material civilization, is now coming to a close. We should all return to the Life way of our ancestors, bringing their gift with us. We must return to our own soul, the native land which is the life principle of Kototama-Futomani. This means standing in **I-WI**, our substance, and looking at universal phenomena. If, from there, we review our material civilization in its totality, the direction of today's society and its institutions would automatically undergo great changes.

When I talk this way, I feel I am making it too difficult for many Budo practicants but I'll continue a little further. My instructors taught me that Budo is neither theory nor intelligence; it must be grasped. They didn't mean an intellectual understanding. If you grasp it, the real movement begins. If what we talk about so nicely cannot be expressed in our physical movement or actions, we may have synthesized what others have told us but this is not Budo. Creating theory or making rationalizations is a study, not Budo. For example, if we try to explain what pain is to someone who has never felt it, using scientific, aesthetic, or religious descriptions, etc., no matter how thorough our explanation is, we can never really convey it. Explanations can create an understanding but not the experience. To experience pain, the body must be struck or cut; there is no other way. To grasp the self or to guide others this way through Budo is a similar situation. We must proceed this way until we arrive at the final objective which is the perfection of humanity.

In the beginning, physical strength, **U**, and technique, **O**, are being guided toward the world of spirit. Budo is, therefore, one of the most important ways in traditional education for perfecting the self, meaning to enter the world of complete freedom. Freedom is happiness, getting past all the limitations of sadness, fear, etc. Everyone knows this intellectually but cannot reach that state of being. Why? It is because no one can get beyond the physical sense experiences, a narrow world where freedom can never be found.

The world of form will inexorably disappear in time. What is realized with the physical senses, in here-now, is truth itself which is then stored in **O** dimension. To do this, each phenomenon must be given a name at the moment of transference. Without a name, we can't keep anything in our memory. The real significance of memory or intelligence is the name of the phenomenon.

The two fold vision of our physical "eye", **U**, and our spiritual "eye", **A**, sees the a priori life world, realizes both finite and infinite phenomena and one by one gives them a name, thus building the **O** dimension world. The process of naming means phenomena are realized and judged separately by **E** dimension's capacity, the source of a posteriori judgment and morality. The **U** dimension world is composed of thousands of separate, individual parts which we see as one reality. This is the limited world. Phenomena act as one continuous thread, interlacing and tying it together. This connecting operation is the capacity of a priori **O**, which creates a posteriori human knowledge.

Human capacity in the order **U E O** realizes, judges and understands the universe in that order and is the way of Amatu Kanagi, the principle of the Kabala. Our scientific-material civilization was created with this principle. The world that is grasped with **A** dimension capacity is very

19

unstable, changing from second to second with the speed of an atom or particle, as seen with the scientific "eye". The desire from **A** is to see all the world of universal life, not just isolated events. Within this unstable world, we grasp something and tie it up in **O** dimension. Standing on the viewpoint of **A-O** and observing **U-O** is called Amatu Sugaso. This order of manifestation is **A O U E** and is responsible for creating religion, philosophy and art.

U E O (scientific view) and **A O U E** (spiritual view) are the two orders or principles of the second civilization which gave guided us for the past eight thousand years. I hope someone will realize here how our second civilization has been searching to clarify and make certain the phenomenal world. This search, however, is blind to the subjective side which realizes the objective phenomenal world. To recognize phenomena there must be a seer to realize it. If we don't understand what this seer is and how it grasps phenomena, there can not be any certainty about its reality. Uncertainty gives rise to different points of view with their respective arguments for which a resolution is never found. Only the Kototama Principle perfectly explains what the seer of phenomena really is. The moment the seer grasps it, at the instant of contact, it should be named directly, coming out in sound as a word. The sense of contact itself is the name. This Word of God which creates civilization and cultivates knowledge by following it, is the order **A I E O U**; Amatu Futonorito Principle.

The **U** of Kanagi and the **A** of Sugaso principles only exist in the objective phenomenal world. The seer grasps from darkness so that the true name of phenomena cannot be given. Without a name, our knowledge cannot develop, so one is arbitrarily given at the moment of realization. Words that evolve in this chaotic way are called hiluko. The sense of the pure seer does not manifest through the sound of hiluko words; the hiluko name expresses a desire contradictory to that of the subject. The seer is the substance of being; being itself. Disregarding this and carelessly naming phenomena, we ourselves are no longer present; the word had no soul and becomes a lie. It is not the name of God nor the word of truth. The object is completely separated from the subject making it impossible for us to have perfect satisfaction or understanding with our words. This viewpoint, which runs counter to the self, is the real cause of my past suffering. The pure subject of myself, life-will, **I**, was being led by my intellect, **O**.

In the practice of martial arts, the moment a partner is about to punch or kick, a beginner sees this with the physical senses. Advanced students, seeing from **A**, are aware of the beginner's mental-spiritual level. The beginner, from **U**, creates a defensive technique in response to his partner's movement; the senior student doesn't focus his mind on calculating a defense but he feels the other's mind and experiences a sense of separateness from "the opponent". This is especially felt when teaching and is not a manifestation of mei-kyou (clean mirror). The viewpoint of these two types of practicants differs significantly. Neither of them is as yet perfect. The final Budo principle is for the student to sense with **A** dimension the opponent's spirit and then leave that feeling behind and perfectly enter the void. This is extremely hard to do during the usual exercise. Grasping the opponent from **U** or **A** means getting stuck on the phenomenon of "opponent". In either case it is a failure even before movement occurs; the spirit has been swallowed up by the power of phenomena.

In Budo, the question of who the winner and loser are is already clear at this moment. Competition in ancient times between two superior Budo practicants didn't necessitate the drawing of swords. Even if swords were drawn, at the moment before the movement, one could feel his spirit drawn away, absorbed by the other, and would concede defeat. In a perfect state of muga, one's mind can not be exhausted or drawn out by the opponent's power and as a result there is no failure. If we think, "Now I am in muga" as we stand before our superior, our mind and spirit will immediately disintegrate. Budo doesn't explain why void is the last step, it only teaches to get it yourself. Zen is the same. After experiencing the void and wondering how it happened, we need the Kototama Principle to see it and be sure.

If we await the opponent with our physical eyes, we are cheated by his technique; if we wait with our "mind", we're cheated by his mind. To reach the final step of Budo, the absolute void, we must continue to practice not being taken by any **U** or **A** dimension phenomena. We must completely lose any sense of winning or defending, losing or dying. We should completely go back to self where the opponent no longer exists. There is no attack or defense; there is nothing! Only the absolute self is there, the life-will **I**, standing in the center of the universal life rhythm in here-now. All universal life energy concentrates and expands in this space; nothing else!

The energy from the one life of the universe acts in a concentrating and expanding direction. As there is synchronization between these energies, automatically there are countless smaller energy whirlpools created in the space of the universe. The human substance also manifests this way; four dimensions of energy having a concentrating direction and four with an expanding direction, making a total of eight motive rhythms. These whirlpools become one part of the universe and are the human substance. Through the action of the eight motive rhythms all necessary elements are collected to create the human body. The action of the four concentrating dimensions is to hold and maintain the elements in the space of the body and the expanding energy manifests in human capacity, both physical and spiritual. The eight motive rhythms are the source of a posteriori power; the unlimited world's manifestation into the limited form of capacity. In ancient religions, this is symbolized as a bridge or rainbow. Ancient Shinto calls it Ameno Ukihasi: "floating bridge in the sky". O Sensei Morihei Ueshiba, the founder of Aikido, grasped the sense of this and his object was to hand it over to his students.

The Budo practicant should ultimately reach this last step which is the perfection of self as a human being. Then his words and actions will benefit the rest of society and awaken the robot-computer beings from their sleep.

---

3. "Eye" of **U** and **A** might be better understood as "radar" or "sensor". Actually, **U** "eye" and **A** "eye" should be more clearly stated as **O** "eye" and **E** "eye". **O** is the eye of night and **E** is that of the day.

From The One Source

The action of a priori **I**, expanding from the "black hole" through the father sounds in all four dimensions, simultaneously, converges into **WI**. This happens instantaneously, for here there is no time and space. From **WI** begins our physical a posteriori life. From the one source our physical senses emerge, each one a separate action from a different group of vibrations. Each sense perceptor, eyes, ears, nose, etc., has its own range. The eyes can only synchronize with those vibrations which produce color and form as we see it; what we hear is in another range and what we smell, yet another one. The eyes cannot catch the vibrations we smell and we can't see shape and color with our nose. The form of life that exists in one sense doesn't exist in another. When we understand the world only in terms of the material, we start from a place after a separation has occurred. We grasp the phenomenal world from five different places which we then try to synthesize in our brain. That is the body's mechanism. We reconstruct from the parts to the whole. We cannot be aware of the one source of our life when we begin with our physical experience of it. We are caught by the body's limitations.

In our daily life, our actions and decisions are based on this limited view. We are influenced by the separation that the mechanism of the body makes in order to experience physical phenomena. Our judgments, morality, laws, etc. all reflect how we see the world through separation. Hence, the mistakes, confusion, and the partial, inadequate solutions that must always be resolved again and again, endlessly, in the wake of new phenomena.

To have perfect judgment, we must search back to the one beginning, to a priori, symbolized as The Garden of Eden. This is our practice; to move from **I** to **WI** and then to see the separate manifestations as they occur in the phenomenal world. We are so convinced that we know something, saying, "I've got it", just from our experience of phenomena, but it's all in pieces, some of which we've no doubt missed.

Often in our practice we confuse these two places. Sometimes we can stay in the, as yet, unformed world of a priori. I don't mean the world of atoms and particles because these are already formed. I mean physical life before it took form, the vibrational dimensions. Even after many years of practice, it is difficult to maintain clarity between these two worlds. It is hard to not cut-off or separate. It's difficult to maintain our confidence in human life as a totality, even though we are obliged to see it separately. We think we're there, that we understand and then suddenly we find ourselves taken by phenomena, crying and complaining having, incredibly,

fallen from heaven to hell. "How could I? I just had it!"
We must continually practice the sound exercises. The
total synchronization is in the fifty sounds that come
from the a priori and manifest in the a posteriori world.
In so doing, we unconsciously put them in order because
we originated in the a priori world. We created the body
and gave it the five sense capacities. Automatically, by
making the sounds, we can regain our original order of
being, re-enter the Garden and synchronize from our life
rhythm to our a posteriori creation. At that time, we can
have perfect judgment.

If we cannot awaken a priori consciousness, our
judgment cannot be complete. If we depend only on our
a posteriori experiences, our original, pure morality
cannot emerge from the chaos of that experience. With a
mind awakened to its a priori capacity, our judgments
and actions will be in order. We cannot be mistaken; at
least, not very much.

When we left the Garden of Eden, we lost the ability to
manifest ourselves as complete human beings. Standing
on a posteriori knowledge, more as robots, we try to
improve our civilization; making "progress" by organizing
it better for everyone's peace and happiness. This is
impossible! We are never able to judge it correctly. We
must start from the pure source of our life. We cannot
see that world intellectually or rationally. The only way
to return is with the fifty sounds.

I cannot impart to you this inner sense of mine; I'm
unable to directly hand it over. I can only tell you about
it. Further, if I've convinced you that what I say is the
truth, you become my slave, my computer, spewing out

what I've put in. The destruction of the Tower of Babel symbolized more than different languages; we became separated from our totality. Without realizing or feeling it, we have become enslaved to a stronger personality.

For instance, you believe you're a pure Buddhist. You've studied from books or a teacher who also studied from books. Buddha never wrote a book. You don't really know what he said because you never met him. However, unknowingly, you've become his robot. His mission was exactly to create this kind of darkness; to hide the life principle, the principle of the Garden of Eden. With the destruction of the Tower of Babel, the fifty sounds were put into symbolic forms. You are willing to die with faith in Buddha, having the certainty of a computer mind, slave to a theory and the symbolic name. Who searches by trying to discover the mind, or the name behind the symbol? How does this name manifest in one's head? Is it the right name, the correct order of sounds? No one uses the true word. The Bible clearly separated the Word of God from that of man.

We are always using the words I AM: **A-I-A-MU**. We must find out where this sound manifests from and what it means. There are as many different types of I am as there are senses, but when we speak we don't clarify which one. Which is the I of "I am free" or "I know"? It was our ancestors' decision to have it this way and we must accept it. However, those who practice must not be blind. The Kototama Principle is here to be grasped, right in our hand, and we must open to it. The others we cannot help unless they too are really searching. They must be sincerely knocking at the door to have it unlocked. With all your good intentions, you must not force people to understand; you'd make them unhappy and you too would suffer. If someone asks, give your all. If they can't receive it, stop! Otherwise, it becomes an act of violence. It's the same in Aikido. When something is coming at you, you synchronize with it. You don't initiate actions which begin from the processing of ideas in the brain. Aikido practice was created to help develop the sense of this. The purpose is to get to the very beginning of ourselves. Others are still trying to clarify in the phenomenal world with their great egos and competitive drive. We must exercise to awaken our own eye of life, to open our own substance.

When we sound out "**TA**" and then "**MA**", we obviously can't make the sounds simultaneously; we must make one sound first. From one sound to the next we create time and space through the capacity of **I** dimension, acting with 8 motive rhythms. The sounds originate from **I** which then synchronizes with physical phenomena and thus creates our sensory experience of the finite world. The inner sense of the sound rhythms created by this synchronization is Mana and as these rhythms are spoken they become Kana, the word of God. It is our own pure capacity as human beings that creates this world. A priori **I** creates all existence in the finite world; this is our own ability. That is why it can be said that we are the creator of the universe. Without realizing this ability to synchronize, you cannot make this statement. If you haven't grasped this yourself, yet say it with a robot head, you're a liar and a criminal. Don't do it that way.

29

About Power

There are many of us who question and search, trying somehow to resolve our inner feelings of chaos. You study different philosophies and religions, turning to art, spiritual exercises, prayer and meditation. Sometimes you think you have it all finally figured out, but then the answers don't stick. The deeper you go, the more difficult the questions become. The intellectual approach doesn't resolve anything satisfactorily. You need to find an answer that is complete and final, which puts all the chaos into some kind of order, so you find a teacher, join a class and it feels like the right way to go. Maybe it's Kototama, Zen or something else. You spend some time seriously practicing and find yourself expecting immediate enlightenment or the mastery of some special power. This is a mistake. There is a general misunderstanding about exactly this, especially among young people.

No one receives instant enlightenment or power, no matter how serious they are. Some historical records might give this impression, but it just isn't so. If something like that did happen to you, it would be very dangerous. You shouldn't expect it.

If we could understand I AM, what it is to be a human being, the manifestation itself of the total universe, it would really be the greatest enlightenment. Nothing can be bigger than the totality; no more magnificent or beautiful.

Maybe after ten years of Zen meditation or our sound exercise, some special awakening will occur, some small enlightenment. However, this is just one part of our manifestation and our human capacity already includes this. It's one small concentration of energy, a minor part of the activity of the universe inside of us. Whatever exercise you're doing, don't hope for anything to happen all of a sudden.

Once, at a summer camp in Ansi, France, I had an experience of that sort. As I was practicing Aikido, I would go "**IEI!**" (Yea) and at that moment there would be strange occurrences; light bulbs would explode and the center mat of the dojo would rise up. One of my students tried to push it down by jumping on it but felt a force pushing back at him. Finally, using his hands with Ki rather than physical strength, he got it to go back. Those students who witnessed the incident were impressed with me as some kind of god-man, in a religious way. It happened several times over a period of six months. I didn't understand it. O Sensei had demonstrated this kind of power in his Aikido. It was a year after his death and he had come to me at times during that period. This power had appeared quite suddenly and continued to occur wherever I went, but it just didn't feel right. I couldn't derive any pleasure from it and I felt unhappy. It was rather frightening, a disagreeable feeling that I can't describe and I felt it was shortening my life. I had studied with mountain practicants and many other teachers in the past, and therefore had a great deal of **O** dimension knowledge. I searched for an explanation and finally realized it was my master's power that he was passing on to me. I sat in meditation and prayed to his soul. I asked his forgiveness saying that I was so grateful for his love in giving it to me, but that I couldn't accept it. I wished to be a normal person, not an extraordinary one. I continued praying for a week until I began to feel lighter inside. Finally the power left me and I felt free.

I can't give any theoretical explanation for what happened. I just didn't like it. I preferred to keep my normal life. The power never came back again. When I had tried to use that power, "**IEI**", with deliberate concentration, nothing happened. Only when I didn't care, when I hadn't been thinking about it and said "**IEI**", is when it came out. I suspect that had I practiced to develop that inner feeling I would have eventually mastered control over it, but all my pleasure in life had been replaced by something else. No thanks!

This is why I ask you not to try to gain some special power. Now that I'm beginning to know who is I AM, that kind of unexplainable power is only a very small part of me. I am the universe, that power was only a small part of universal energy, concentrating and expanding inside of me. Acquiring power is no different from taking a pill; why should I be interested?

Why is this so misunderstood? The underlying reason is a personal desire for superiority over other human beings. Seeking to be superior is a mistake right from the start. If you get it, it will destroy you. It is a twisted, unbalanced vibration for human life; not the pure, final power. It's true that some people have strong and special powers; visionaries, clairvoyants and the like. However, it isn't necessary. It's a limited power, just one small, strong point of concentration and it is always accompanied by a physical handicap or some other abnormality; some contraction. Ueshiba Sensei, though, was quite normal. He told us he had the spirit of his dragon god. For me, the power was unpleasant.

Don't fool yourself about your real motivation. You must not lie to yourself or to others because you then lie to the earth, plants, animals and the entire universe. Without knowing who is I AM, what it is to be a human being, you haven't the final answer. Ask some great and famous man who he is or who you are and if he can't give a clear answer, he's a liar! This question alone is enough to show you where he is.

The first words of a human being are I AM; this is the beginning of language. You may know all about this intellectually. You can give an **O** dimension answer: in which dimension of I AM, changing in here-now, all of the I AM's, the fifty sounds, all five dimensions, ten rhythms...you could repeat everything I've said which would mean you're also a liar! To be truthful, you must see it clearly in your own manifestation, with your own confidence. This part is difficult, to see how you manifest fifty sounds and how the five dimensions act together. In a posteriori we can see only one dimension at a time, therefore we can't see how all the actions happen at once. My explanation isn't your own; you are still blind. You must be sure before you say I AM for everything is based on it.

Everyone lies when they say I AM, without seeing themselves. You must know what you're doing; that is the way of the truth. When we ate from the Tree of Knowledge it was a crime and we were thrown out of the Garden of Eden. When we act from only an ego-oriented, intellectual understanding, we are condemned to suffer in this hell-world. All of these symbolic explanations are so beautifully stated in stories like the Tower of Babel, Noah's Ark, etc. Our ancestors were really tremendous. Who can create such perfect symbols now? It proves they must have had a complete understanding of the Kototama Principle. Latter-day people have had revelations but couldn't judge what kind of spiritual power was helping them, causing the mistaken explanations they gave to others. Their prophecies have been all mixed up because they didn't have the eye of the Kototama; they were only able to catch something through the capacity of their **A** dimension. There are no mistakes in the symbols left to us over eight thousand years ago by our most ancient ancestors.

Today everyone comes from their **O** dimension with just a sense of opening to **A**. Inside the body is still in **O**, like a seed first sprouting, just starting to see **A** but with most of it still underground. These people believe they're very spiritual. Someday the seed will become a big tree, but you can't help by forcing it before its time.

So don't be mistaken in your estimation of where you are;

there is still a very long way to go. If your interest is in obtaining special powers, you will surely lose your way.

Reflections While Fishing

When you make free sounds, two or three will come to mind very quickly and you'll prefer one over the others. Let the first one come out! If you start thinking it over you'll become confused. The sounds that follow will come from a tightened mind because you've made an intellectual choice. Take that very first sound, whether you like it or not; it doesn't matter. You must manifest directly from head to mouth. Don't let the sounds go back to your head first or you will not improve. Everyone is using the fifty sounds every time they speak, only it's not clear. It's a matter of putting them in order through comparison with the Futonorito order. You must be free to let them come out and admit where you are at that moment - and not care!

This exercise becomes very clear in Budo, especially in Kendo, where the physical action must follow the moment. If there is any hesitation or slight confusion, if

37

you are thinking of the technique, it doesn't work. The thoughts that interfere with instantaneous action are called "mayoi". Making free sounds is analogous to putting down the first brush-stroke when painting; afterwards, we can reflect on its quality. All these exercises are based on practiced spontaneity; it must be a free exercise.

Yesterday I went fishing overnight. My mind was in such a state that I was ready to abandon my original objective in coming to Santa Fe. I had given up on Asia and Europe after having worked so hard there. Santa Fe was my last hope for housing a center which could serve as a guide for the upcoming third civilization. I wanted to help save the world from the hell of this second civilization; to help release mankind from slavery. However, it didn't go so well, particularly with this organization. The members didn't understand my objective and I couldn't make it clear to them. So many things happened that slowly I lost my courage, nearly losing the way of my mission. I had become weak in my struggle with the phenomenal world and I was ready to give up the mission and resume my private life. This would mean separating my actual physical life from the order of Amatu Hitsugi. Here I admonish you not to lose your courage to phenomenal events, as I had nearly lost mine. There were so many reasons, but they were all from the world of phenomena.

When fishing, I was in a natural place, within the vibration of natural surroundings, and slowly my courage revived. Upon reflection, I decided I would carry on even if all of you left. What meaning would my life have if I just continued a comfortable robot existence? I decided to throw everything out and return to myself. How could I have been so mistaken? There can be so much pressure and confusion from actual society that I no longer felt any pleasure from it. I had gradually tightened up and couldn't see my way. In human society, there is nothing to give me courage; only the devil to destroy my life. I decided that it couldn't be that way! Why should human society be smaller than the natural environment? Why is it that only in nature life is pure? Why doesn't this exist among human beings? We say we are superior, but really we are the worst. In order to expand human society, we must bring it back to its original place in the universe.

I had thought of Santa Fe as the world center for this change. That is why I came here and I had nearly lost my courage. Having this hope was a big mistake. You cannot put your last hope in anything. The way of Amatu Hitsugi has no beginning or end. I should have just gone ahead alone. Having hope is an **A** dimension activity and we will always be mistaken. That is why, in the Kototama Principle, we talk about the devil in **A**; "Acuma". If you take **A**, it will kill you. The **O** sound in "hope" can't be correct because the word itself refers to something in the future, which is **A** dimension. What is meant by "hope" includes the imagination and the desire that comes from **A** dimension.

When I left everything behind in Europe to come here, I had great expectations. However, it has been a struggle and my personal life is becoming smaller, as it had in Europe after having the same hope there. Again I felt my life was being pushed down in the same way. Even the happiness of **A** dimension was gone. The story had repeated itself. Hope was gone and now there was no place else to go. I have no interest in the desert or to speak to people there, unless they wish to see me. Without rocks, trees and water, I don't think my a posteriori life could enjoy anything there. Even at the thought, I lose interest in doing such a thing.

I could return to Japan. Traditionally, this country holds the Kototama Principle. It is in the language and they already know the name Kototama. However, their **O** dimension has completely twisted the meaning of the fifty sounds. It feels very heavy to talk to them as they've already been taught it in a different way. When you say **O** or **A**, they have already given it a meaning that is hard to change; they already "know". It would be too difficult for them to find the real meaning of the sounds and I would have a much harder time there.

As for other countries, I don't care to start learning Spanish or Chinese or some other language at this late date. India alone has two hundred different languages. What can I do? If I can't continue my mission here then I would just finish my a posteriori life in this place and be resigned that it didn't come out.

Now, however, I can see clearly that I shouldn't struggle anymore with the phenomenal world. Unconsciously, I was losing my power and becoming smaller. No more! I'll continue to go my way. My biggest mistake was my **A** dimension, my hope, and as a result, my disappointment. With each person I would have new hope and, realistically, it wouldn't happen. Now I don't care. Whatever develops in you, however much you grow or lose ground, I won't bother about it anymore; either way! I'll do my best and whether it comes out or not doesn't matter. I want to be alone. When I ask you to help in my work, it's not for me personally but because it's the only way to save humanity. There is no shame in that. Everyone should help me! The Kototama Principle is the biggest and final one. I could become angry, questioning why you don't understand but it's no use! It depends on each person's present capacity. If someone can't help, it's because it is not yet their time. Later, that person may be able to help ten times more; in the time of Amatu Hitsugi. I'm clear now and I won't lose my courage.

Those were my reflections while fishing. To make the Kototama Principle clear in our own life there are many ways to practice. This morning, I gave you some examples of how to practice but there are so many. You must continue to reflect yourselves, to see what dimension you are struggling with; why you have fear, anger, etc.

It was Friday evening and we had planned to continue fishing at the marina all night. It was so quiet there with just a few people around, enjoying the stillness. At about 10:30 a boat came with a radio blaring. We were all there to escape from civilization, to return to natural sounds. It was terrible! There were four young people and they had no idea what they were doing to us. Some people left, but my wife and I remained. They were fishing and they gradually settled near us. They started speaking to my wife but she couldn't understand their English, so she didn't answer. Their laughter frightened her. It was at that moment the fish started biting, but my wife didn't seem happy and I realized she was afraid. So I gave it up, just as the fish had begun to bite. It made no sense if we both couldn't enjoy it.

The next morning I inquired of my wife about it. She said she felt bad, but their manner of speaking was too difficult for her to understand. I asked her why she had been afraid as they were just other human beings. She said, "My imagination was scaring me more and more. I didn't answer them and perhaps they'd feel offended and get angry with me for insulting them." At the bottom of fear however, lies **O** dimension. Imagination, from **A** dimension, isn't what makes one afraid. In her **O** dimension, my wife had remembered stories of unruly young people, like motorcycle gangs, doing violence to others for a small offense or even just for kicks. "That's what made you afraid", I said. We talked about **A** and **O** working simultaneously in her head, not one first and then the other, but at the same time. That's why I say all four dimensions act together to create our a posteriori capacity. We focus from moment to moment on whichever dimension is strongest. One must see the manifestation first. Her imagination, **A**, was working most strongly but had they not been young and rough in appearance, she wouldn't have been afraid. What she held in her **O** dimension about such people made her fear them. As her **O** dimension had gotten bigger, so had her fear. There are two I AM's and in one of them fear doesn't exist. She had separated into two.

She and I always practice this way; questioning each other, thereby making it clear for ourselves. This is the right way to educate children as well. Their **O** dimension is not so thick and they can understand more easily. Teachers may be more comfortable to just talk about the past, civilization's **O** dimension, but this kind of education isn't helpful for children; it becomes harder for them. In my own case, I'd become stuck in the U-**O** dimension and small things bothered my head. Society is so upside-down and I had allowed my head to become upside-down, too.

First be clear who is I AM, and once you've got it, don't lose it. Be careful because it can also be dangerous. I believe that I'm alone in the world and I must show others the way. How strong I have been in my resolve, yet I could be reduced to this! When you travel the way of truth, you must be strong and not lose yourself in phenomenal changes. We are completely separated from the natural world rather than living in harmony with it. This is our mission as human beings, the synchronization of our society. Who can understand the way of truth? We must go on. Only in this civilization are we so alienated from nature; since we started building houses instead of resting on the earth. No other dimension's world is so separated as is ours; all the others live in peaceful harmony. We made a special place apart for ourselves. It's not the way! We think in our **O** dimension that we can live on earth and ignore it; that everything else can be sacrificed to us to make our lives perfect. Nonsense!

Once you're interested in the Kototama Principle, you've taken one part of the mission for the purification of the world. You need to have pure confidence and belief in the human substance; not in **A** dimension. Even I, at my age, with all my confidence and courage, can still wander. So now I've explained it all to you, showing the right way to go.

43

Truth and Reality

To speak is the first action. What is our understanding of the word "truth"? When you speak, do you search this way, asking these kinds of questions? "Truth" doesn't mean the same thing in each person's **O** dimension, but it is commonly agreed upon to be something that is higher and purer. It's actual meaning is **TU-LU-U-SU: TU** - the beginning of the manifestation of physical senses; **LU** - turning around with the physical senses; **U** - in a dark place; **SU** - concentrating, trying to see in a dark world. Using this word to describe your actual desire makes you a liar. You are lying to yourself as your desire is not **TU-LU-U-SU**. You seek for this because you feel tired of the world and its suffering and wish to see the "truth". That's why there is trouble; the action of the sounds searches for the light, with the physical senses, in a dark, chaotic place. What comes out is different from your real desire, therefore it's not what you meant. The real meaning of the word is opposite to its intellectual definition, to which we add our hope and imagination, like becoming more pure, etc. There is a big difference between the idea and what you are actually saying. That's why we must complete the fifty sounds of the Kototama and find the meaning of the word.

Reality: **LI-A-LI-TI**- the light of life **LI**, lighting up **A**, coming out to the physical senses and again going back. **LI-TI** to see inside, remaining at the bottom. You say, "This is the truth; I'm sure it is right." Your inner desire is to express the meaning behind the sounds **LI-A-LI-TI**, reality, but by your sounds you are not saying that. You use the word "truth". You lie to yourself and it follows that you must lie to others. I follow your language in order to communicate with you, although I know the difference in the meaning of the sounds and the words used. To know, makes mine a bigger crime than one who doesn't know. Buddha says that when you need to give society back its life, you can lie if it helps to guide them towards salvation. You can see how well our ancestors understood the Kototama Principle.

LI-A-LI-TI: to come from **I**, light up from **A**, go back to the life rhythm **LI** and act out and see the source of life **TI**. Everyone wishes to return to that place. There is a great discrepancy between our desires and the language we use. We seek the truth when we mean reality. Without knowing, how can we judge a crime? We must change our language. Everyone is searching for something deeper and more pure, that which we call truth. We're tired of the cheating and confusion, the suffering in our society, but we can't see why it's become this way. Our society exerts a negative pressure on our daily lives and people can't tolerate it anymore. Our life-will cannot accept this civilization but no one tries to see which dimension's judgment is acting, telling us that it's not the right way. **IE** dimension is beginning to awaken inside of us, especially among young people. Whatever they try to do in the world always turns out to be a disappointment. They actively seek the truth yet continually fall short of their goal. Their life becomes more like the animal's existence; the "hippie" with no home and no money. They're searching for the "truth" but if they said instead, " I must find reality", things would change. It's even better to say, "I must see and take back the way of reality." We create words and live in that dimension's world. Once we've created a type of civilization, we remain within the boundaries of that dimension.

You try to find your own manifestation in its perfect order, that is, the name of god, Koto. If you don't know what you're doing, what can your activity accomplish? How can you trust the activity coming from the language belonging to your **O** dimension when it is so far removed from your inner desire? Trust: **TU-LA-SU-TU**; you're just playing the fool with each other when you use this word. Believe (Be-lie-ve) translated back into pure sounds is **HI-LI-FU**. Note the difference between the sounds in trust and believe.

Language is the father of civilization and the letter is its mother. We must try to see this clearly or else we can't progress any further. The language of **U** dimension creates an **U** dimension civilization, **O** creates a civilization based on **O** dimension, etc. That's why language is the father. We must recall our language from the world of **IE** dimension, the word or name of god, which was the language of our ancestors over eight thousand years ago. The mission of our ancestors, Jesus,

47

Buddha, Fu-I (I-Ching), Shen Nung (Natural Medicine), etc., was to hide the word, changing it to a lower dimension, which wasn't easy. It is now time for us to purify our language and raise it again to a higher dimension, a mission directly opposite from theirs.

All the world must become one country and speak the same language. After the destruction of the Tower of Babel, there was no longer any communication among peoples and they separated into various groups which then went different ways. Later, these groups couldn't communicate with each other because they had created different languages. To use the Kototama fifty sounds, you must have the name of god. We must return to the time of Moses for his was the mission responsible for hiding the word, not David or any of the later ones. The whole world, not just the Jews, must go back eight thousand years. Since the time when the Kototama was hidden, all elements of society have been existing without their root. This also holds true for natural therapy and is why it doesn't have a complete theoretical framework today. In order for it to become clear, we must return to a time previous to eight thousand years ago. What we have now is all from the lower dimensions.

The events of daily life are questions for your practice. Don't be too lazy to reflect on them. You say, "I trust you, I love you...," but don't reflect on what you're saying. As a serious student you can never purify if you don't start here, with the sounds. Otherwise, your physical life weakens, you lose hope and then it's finished! Only Kototama members can save society from the hell world, but we also fall down to physical desire. Already we feel proud in teaching others what we know, yet our daily life is only a matter of satisfying **U** dimension, the lowest desires. It's very sad. You have a chance, but you can't see nor hear this. In your heart, you can't come to my meaning; instead you just spend your time pursuing desires from **U**. If you want to save yourself, you can't stay there.

Borrowed Knowledge

At this moment, I'm in darkness; I don't see anything new. This is your responsibility because you are not seeing anything new. It is all a manifestation from our substance. When one person sees new things, everyone who is searching can get it. When I experience darkness it means you are not opening. It's true! When you're not searching or paying attention, the spark of a new thing will pass away. I don't mean seeing things, phenomena, in the light of **A** dimension. To catch the spark, we must feel it as our own manifestation. Science sees phenomena from the **U** dimension viewpoint. The serious practicant sees phenomena from **A** dimension, but this is not yet being in **A**. To see that which comes from the light of **A** is not yet the Kototama world because it is still phenomena and you are separated from it. Phenomena exist there and are appearing to me here; that makes two. You are not yet in Heaven Country.

In Heaven Country there are no phenomena because it is the moment of our own manifestation. You cannot realize this without the Kototama Principle. When we see something in the physical world we remember the experience and store it in our memory. In the same manner, when we have an **A** dimension experience, this also becomes a part of our **O** dimension. Based on our experienced memory we believe that we "know". This is not complete, however; it is not yet the truth. If you already think you know, you're not interested in making any effort to search more deeply. You can't, because you're already convinced you've found it and you resist anyone trying to guide you to a deeper place. You continue to turn around in **A** and **O** dimension feeling sure that you have the truth.

The goal of Ohsawa Sensei, the founder of macrobiotics, was to guide all humanity to the Yin-Yang principle so that they could attain the highest judgment. Recently, I received a letter from the director of a macrobiotic center. The man I received the letter from had studied for ten years with Michio Kushi, a disciple of Ohsawa. For him, the Yin-Yang principle has become a new religion, **A** experience stored in **O**. I don't think he's had much experience curing sick people with macrobiotics, not in any intimate way. To do this, you must stay with the patient all the time and prepare his food. Otherwise, it's just a theory you've studied to which you add some of your own ideas. One needs the experience of actually healing people this way. Ohsawa had asked his members to know how to prepare food as medicine. Students of Michio Kushi are mostly talking and writing instead. Each patient must have a different diet designed for his particular condition, as I practiced in India. This man criticized an article I'd written because in it I said macrobiotic practitioners are not careful enough about climate and geographical differences in their diagnosis and treatment. (He understood me to say that they did not take them into consideration at all!)

Today, when people eat, they don't think enough about where they are living. For instance, when we eat tropical fruits, these are foods that don't grow here because their elements cannot withstand this climate. When you eat them, the body gathers these elements to produce new cells, continuously. If we live in the tropics and eat those fruits it is in harmony with the environment, but eating them here makes our cells weak. We are changing our body's constitution for tropical conditions, yet remaining here. The effect is a loss in the body's ability to maintain balance and then disease can develop. This is Ohsawa's teaching and, roughly, his students know this. However, they are not really making any serious calculations, such as the variation in the quantity of water used in cooking rice between Santa Fe, Boston and California. There is quite a difference in preparation due to the varying dry and humid conditions. For reasons such as these I had said they weren't paying enough attention.

I have thirty years of experience and he with his ten years offers to instruct me. I followed Ohsawa from India to Europe, leaving my family behind in Japan. He wants to teach me, yet his teacher is my contemporary. Another disciple and old friend, Mr. Nakamura, wrote to me from West Germany. He said he's suffering terribly, trying to fathom the meaning of Yin-Yang. It's the basis of macrobiotics and he feels he's lost it, unable to see it anymore. Before, when we were studying with Ohsawa, we understood the theory in our O dimension. Ohsawa said Yin expands and Yang concentrates. We memorized what he said without examining it; just believing it. We believed that if people ate and prepared food according to his principles, human capacity would be developed to reach its highest judgment, and from there a peaceful world would be established.

Everywhere we went if we saw a sick person, we would approach him and offer to help. "Please listen to me!", we said. We tried to force the diet on people. Were we not on a mission? People would respond in anger, "Who are you to talk to me about my illness?" We insisted, saying "I'm telling you the truth! If you don't listen, you're a devil, and a criminal." I had no shame or guilt about speaking in such violent tones. Many religious people proselytize in this way and it has become like this for those who practice macrobiotics also.

I strictly followed the diet for many years. First, I ruined my own health and that of my wife. My younger son, who was on the diet from infancy, was so lacking in calcium we had to keep his pelvic area in a cast for six months. So severely did I follow the diet, so seriously did I care for patients, that I could not see the situation quite clearly. Finally, I found many incongruencies. The very meaning of the words "Yin" and "Yang" was mistaken. It was Ohsawa's incorrect interpretation of the meaning of Yin and Yang that led to an erroneous theory which he tried to put into practice with food preparation. Nevertheless, he did promulgate the eating of natural food and that alone can help.

It also helped that no one was able to prepare food perfectly, to the exact specifications of the theory, especially when they cooked at home without a teacher supervising them. So there were those more casual followers of macrobiotics who did benefit from the diet and could effect a cure. The sick ones who seriously followed the diet are all dead.

I was in India, north of Madras, at the Universal Institute, where I ran a hospital. Every day I cooked for forty or fifty people and from those experiences I got answers to my questions! I went to see Ohsawa in France. He had just come from Africa where he had tried unsuccessfully to convince Dr. Schweitzer of his ideas concerning diet. We met in Paris whereupon I explained my experiences in India. At that time, we had only one way of cooking; that which was appropriate to Japan. I divided it into four categories and lessened the salt intake. He conferred ranks in macrobiotics, the highest one being the fifth, and only five people in the world had received that rank. He ranked me seventh. He was really pleased with his most superior student and he immediately divided the diet into seven categories and reduced the salt.

It doesn't matter that I received seventh dan ranking. This man, a director with ten years of experience, by his judgment writes to me saying he'd be glad to answer any questions I might have. I ask you not to do such a shameful thing. When you talk or write to someone, you must know exactly who that person is before you offer to answer his questions. Don't assume they know less than you. I don't think this man ever treated patients directly with food preparation. He has only an intellectual understanding and hasn't put the theory into practice. If you are not curing people as your patients, you have only a theoretical understanding of macrobiotics.

How could you say you know Aikido in theory? If you don't have the power in practice and try to teach others, it's like teaching from a book. It's the same in our schools. For example, an acupuncture teacher cannot maintain his practice so well, therefore he becomes a professor. What caliber of students comes out of his classes? Western medical schools work the same way.

I feel sad for the man who wrote this letter. He has no idea how shameful it was for him to have written to me that way. He'll treat everyone like that and have no shame for himself. Our members must never make such an awful error. It's as if after studying at a theological seminary, you write a letter to Jesus telling him, "You don't know anything about Christianity so I'll teach you. I've been a Christian for ten years. If you have any questions, ...etc." This shows you're absolutely blind by your arrogance and pride in the knowledge you store in your memory. Having a large number of photographs is nothing to be proud of; you're only a collector. It's like being an art collector, knowing nothing about painting but telling the artist how to paint and if he has any questions you'd be glad to answer them. You know because you've collected a whole lot of paintings.

This man addressed the letter to Third World instead of Third Civilization. How could he have mistaken this when there is such a big difference in their meanings? From the beginning he showed his foolishness. Be careful, whatever you do, your mistakes reveal your own poverty of mind. Why was it necessary for him to demonstrate his poor judgment and shamefulness? It is pitiful that he's in the position of a director.

No matter how much you love other people and try to help them, don't be misguided. You'll kill the name of Kototama, the other side of the name Jehovah God; Amatu Hitsugi. It's your arrogance that dirties the name and it will become a heaviness in your life. It's your own pure self, your own substance which you are doing this to. You can't make it dirty or shameful because if you do, you can't save yourself.

I could go on all day about this but I'm not saying anything new. Our exercise is to see the action of the fifty sound rhythms, to make sure who is I AM. If you can't make it clear, how can we talk about it? In Japan, traditionally, they say, "Don't talk, do it." We don't trust or respect a person who speaks well; the one who can act is respected as a leader. The armchair general is obliged to lose in a real war. Our real capacity is not our **O** dimension intelligence. This is only one part of our capacity. First, the question is, can you do it? Your actions reflect your spirit. Beware of speaking with someone else's knowledge as your own, like the fox who borrows the tiger's skin.

Awakening
to Human Life

Note the difference in the order of sounds between
Futonorito and Sugaso; **TI KI SI HI** (Sugaso) and **TI KI
MI HI** (Futonorito). Tonight we practiced the sounds
from the subjective side of the five dimensions. Then we
sounded out **U-A-WA**. From **U**, **A** divides subject and
object and then comes **O E**. The objective side is **WA
WO WE**. **I** is the subject, **WI** is the object or the
physical aspect so in Futonorito order, the **I** side is **TI KI
MI HI** and **LI NI YI SI** belongs to **WI**. In Sugaso order,
the subjective side is **TI KI SI HI** and **YI MI LI NI** is
the objective part. With respect to the subjective side, **TI
KI** is the same in both orders but in one case **MI** is on the
subjective side, and in the other it is part of the objective
aspect.

When we take the order **TI KI SI HI** it is the Sugaso
way. If we manifest in the order **KI SI TI NI** (subject),
HI MI YI LI (object) we take the Kanagi way. In both

59

cases we say, "This is my own way; I'm absolutely sure it is right." Right or left side, you are confident that your manifestation is correct. Manifesting in a posteriori, we are obliged to take one of three ways; that's how the world divides itself. No matter how powerfully the Kototama Principle manifests in the future, when the world recognizes this principle, human interest will still divide three different ways. It is unavoidable. However, the way of truth is Futonorito order. Both Sugaso and Kanagi orders are paths leading to the creation of crime: **KU-LA-I-MU**. **KU** means to manifest with the physical senses, **LA** is expanding, turning around and expanding, **I** is the Life-Will, the source. **KU-LA** cannot see **I**, it's own substance, therefore **KU-LA-I** means it's absolutely dark. **MU** is based on **MI**; it is **MI** manifesting in the physical senses. One cannot see anything from **U** dimension before the division to **A-WA**. Nothing has been formed or named when we are still in **U**. A-Om-Mu, as it is said in Indian Yogic tradition, means returning back to the source of nothing. At the end of **A** dimension there is the void, you cannot go any further. This is exactly what quantum physics is finding, that at the end of breaking apart and separating phenomena they arrive at nothing. (It is also a crime to explain each father sound to you without letting you find it yourself).

The sound **MI** forms something or goes to look, which implies that it has already manifested physically. If there's no form, you can't be looking at it. In the Yamato language, **MI-LU** means "looking at". In the activity of this father rhythm, **MI** (the sense of it) becomes **MU**; seeing what has manifested through **U** dimension. Since **MU** has no form yet, nothing can be seen. **KU-LA-I-MU** means that you don't have **I**, yourself. It is total darkness. What can you see turning around with energy in a dark place? The word "crime" means you can't find your own substance, **I**. In this state, not being able to see or grasp the source of yourself and moving around in the dark, you create something. It's sure to be something convenient and comfortable because it is based on physical experience. You move the stone that is in your way in order to make a road. You create a civilization that's oriented towards more comfort and convenience. The crime is letting human beings create this kind of civilization.

However, to explain each sound to you is not quite right. Each sound has a much wider meaning than what has been given so far. **MU**, for instance, is not limited to what I have said about it. If you memorize what I'm saying, putting it in your **O** dimension, you will only have a limited understanding of the sounds. That's no use; it won't help you emerge from this hell-world. You've come here to study and practice, to find salvation for your a posteriori life. You listen to me and then put it all in your **O** dimension because you don't see anything else. This isn't the right way to help you open up; you must do it for yourselves. I've explained some of it to you, but what's needed is to break through to an inner feeling which must be done by yourself.

Once you become a Kototama practicant, you should not talk so much but rather, let your actions speak for you. Talking makes you a fool and you find yourself on a path you never meant to take. It is better not to talk at all. For seven years now I've been talking and explaining, but no one understands, or grasps it, although many believe they have. No one has been able to open from the bottom;

awakening their own life's flower. You have an **O** dimension understanding but your life hasn't blossomed yet. What is a Kototama practicant if you can't open up? You listen to my explanation and you store it in your mind like some secret knowledge. This is not the Kototama! Even worse than that! For example, let's take the case of the young man from Boston. He came to only a few classes and is now teaching the Kototama at the East-West Foundation. When he was here, some of you were very kind to him, offering him a place to stay, finding him a job, etc. When he left, he didn't say thank you or even a good-bye to anyone. Now he writes and phones us, seeking our cooperation and asking elementary questions. He doesn't even have it in his **O** dimension. He uses the name Kototama, saying it's the best and explaining it to everyone. He can't say thanks or good-bye, but now he lectures in Boston. He also claims to understand the meaning of the Messiah's return: To To Ko Ko, like some mystical revelation he's found. Our ancestors searched a million years for the fifty sound principle; he came four times and can talk about it.

It has taken all of humanity's energy over the last five thousand years to arrive at our present scientific understanding. Suppose that someone spent four hours in a science class, having known absolutely nothing prior and now talks about atomic theory like an expert. Imagine how ludicrous his ideas would be? How many years does a scientist spend with his studies, backed by the knowledge of thousands of years? Even still, that kind of learning is not as difficult as the Kototama Principle because it can be seen and studied with the physical senses.

If I had never spoken the name Kototama, this young man couldn't have either. The crime is not so much his as my own. Now he acts as if he were the American representative of the Kototama, teaching it in Boston. Even after having spent many years with me, there are those who still see what I say as a kind of philosophy and make their own understanding of it. They say, "Now I know, so it's time to leave!" They never understood at all. They tried to appropriate my understanding as their own. I have said before and will say again that you can't study the Kototama from someone else. You must manifest yourself as a complete human being. To do this you need countless exercises for studying and searching inside yourself.

Of course, when I say that it's not something to be studied, people always mistake my meaning. They will say, "I don't have to know anything, I can just manifest myself. I don't need anybody, I can practice alone." It invariably gets turned around to be the opposite of what I've said. Do you think you can get out of **O** dimension by yourself? It is the arrogance of **O** dimension that causes you to think so. All the great founders of religions, Buddha, Jesus, etc. suffered so much through hard exercises, not caring if they died along the way, only being dedicated to their search. That's why they were such powerful leaders. Those without discipline, who find excuses for their physical existence with their sentimentality, and who base their decisions from those desires, will never get it, no matter how intelligent they are. To really open up you must be willing to die, not in the sense of suicide, but to not care about physical or emotional suffering, money problems, etc. It means to throw it all out and just keep on searching.

You must put your complete confidence in opening up and manifesting Futonorito order. This is my own way of practice! Whatever problems and difficulties arise do not matter; it will all be arranged. If you can't do it, falling down to sentiment, physical comfort or pressures for social status and success, then you just become a normal person living in this epoch. Nothing more, nothing less. When you open to your total capacity, you become the Messiah. Who else can do this for you? It won't come up out of the earth or from heaven! Jesus and Moses were not supermen; they manifested with a human body, not something else. To open your own complete humanity means your a posteriori capacity would be like theirs.

There are so many strong, intelligent people but unfortunately no one is serious enough to reawaken their self. They all succumb to the lower desires of their daily life, like **A** dimension sentiment and dreams. Perhaps the highest capacity from our **A** dimension in society today is intuition, but there are not so many of those that have manifested this ability who can base their life on this or inspiration alone. Most people live from their physical senses combined with a little **A** dimension emotion and imagination. They move around that way and can't see how pitiful they are. They think that's all there is to life and to being human, but it's not so!

So don't talk about it. Just awaken inside yourself. It is a matter of human life, but it is hard to understand.

The Civilization
of "Ladies First"

It is written in the Kojiki that Izanagi and Izanami had a conversation about creating civilization. They started searching by going in opposite directions around the column of heaven. When they met on the other side, Izanami spoke first, resulting in the creation of "hiluko", or child without bones. "Hone" means the sound of **I**, so hiluko is a child without hone or **I** dimension. If **I** dimension is not able to manifest, the sound **IE** cannot come out. This is a mythological story about a god and goddess which tells us, in metaphor, what actually occurs in our own lives, right now.

Izanagi is **A-LE**, a priori **A** dimension and Izanami is **WA-LE**, physical, a posteriori life. When **WA-LE**, physical phenomena, speaks first, standing in the place of the subject and **A-LE** speaks after, we can not get hone. We can only produce hiluko and are therefore unable to make perfect child sounds. In other words, our search of

65

the principle is so difficult because in our exercises, even when we think we're standing in **A**, we automatically stand on the **WA** side, always looking at phenomena first.

The god and goddess didn't destroy the child; they put it into a reed boat and placed it in the river. Thus, hiluko language was taught to "outside" countries, called Yomotsu-kuni. In a particular Shinto ceremony, they still make a paper baby and put it into the river.

Izanagi and Izanami went back to Takamahala to ask the ancestors what had gone wrong; that is, they went searching their a priori. They had tried to create this country (kuni), or civilization, in order to better the conditions of physical life. They wanted to create a civilization that was complete. The ancestors explained that the woman spoke first and that they must return to earth and circle the column again, which they did. This time Izanagi spoke first, and later the woman. In this way they succeeded in producing a perfect child which is the complete country; the fifty sounds symbolically.

For the man to speak first means to begin from the a priori or the **A-LE** side. If we stand on the side of phenomena, woman first, we can not get it. Traditional Japanese etiquette always puts the man first and the woman after so that they do not make hiluko. They don't know why they do this because they've lost the principle, but this is where it comes from. Western civilization originally followed the Hebrew tradition and it was not until the "Age of Chivalry" that the custom of "ladies first" was initiated.

At our core, we cannot find the "ladies first" idea

acceptable because we know what it really means. This may also account for a certain historical hostility in the West toward women that begins with Eve. Woman is the embodiment of the frustration of our inner desire for self-realization. Our resistance to this civilization, which puts phenomena first, is expressed in this way.

In our search to enter Eden we are obliged to stand on the **A-LE** side, no matter how difficult it is. We cannot place Izanami as the subject or else all our ideas and understandings are born from hiluko and everything becomes a mistake. It seems simple to understand this in our **O** dimension civilization, but moving with this current and this language, it is very hard to return to our original humanity. When practicing, be very careful to see which side of you manifests first.

It's hard to realize, but **A-LE** means we are no longer in **O** dimension. We are so used to standing in **O**, actually **WO**, having phenomena (Izanami) in our minds first and then trying to understand them. That is **O-LE**. In the Japanese language, A-le, Wa-le and O-le all mean I AM. To start with **A-LE** means to come from nothing; no ideas and no desires. It then comes in to **O** dimension. The usual route our mind takes begins with knowledge from **AO** or **UO**, the manifestation of the lower parts of ourselves. **U** dimension is the way of science which is now almost complete. **A** dimension is much less developed. It's mostly emotion with a little imagination and a bit of inspiration. Our **O** dimension separates **UO** and **AO** because neither side is as yet complete. Both sides must be finished before they can meet:

Whichever direction we take around the column of

heaven, the problem is the same.
Izanami speaking first means a
civilization that is led by scientific
knowledge; the civilization of
"ladies first". In this order
(Kanagi) the spiritual side is weak.

Our personal life is the same as the current we live in. You can see that this is a Kanagi based civilization, judging it intellectually from the outside. What you cannot see is how you do the same thing in your daily life. You imagine you are already in Eden, a god-man, but just watch yourself, your ideas, how your mind works and what you do! It's very hard to get it and everyone is obliged to suffer the purification of five thousand years of karma. It's even heavier when you're Jewish because your karma includes a physical lineage going back to those ancestors who took the responsibility for developing Kanagi civilization through language, education and prophecy.

It's so simple - only fifty sounds! We can even memorize them! Our ancestors spent thousands, perhaps millions of years, to complete them. We've been given the answer directly, but how are we to apply it to life's daily questions? It is difficult but this is our work; to practice using the complete answer as a mirror. There are so many questions. Which answer applies to which situation? Even with much more practice and experience it remains difficult. Nevertheless, we are obliged to go ahead without being afraid to suffer because it is our purification and there is no other way. Otherwise, all our confusion will follow us. No one can help you! It must come out in you, through your exercise. You must give back to yourself the perfect answers. I, too, have such heavy questions and wonder how to apply the answers, yet it's all there in the fifty sounds. We can't find it, however, by trying to use the Kototama mirror from the Izanami side (**O** dimension, **WA-WO**). We cannot reflect from the side of **WA-LE**, the I am based on physical senses, because as it becomes the subject and faces the phenomenal world, it cannot see Izanagi.

Izanagi and Izanami are absolutely one! Our knowledge must be exactly the same as the order of our activity, no longer separating. **AO** dimension is only spiritual expansion; **UEO** is just the knowledge of our physical senses as they face the finite world. Neither of these are complete. **AIEO** is the knowledge from the creator of human life. Spiritually, it is symbolized as the great god Izanagi and his physical counterpart, the goddess Amaterasu-ohomi-kami, but actually it is our own substance.

Still, we separate Izanagi and Izanami. We cannot make it one. This means Izanami can't follow the order of Izanagi; Izanami always speaks first. However much you try to concentrate and be one with your sounds, Izanami always appears as ideas and phenomena. If you just do the sounds mechanically, from **O** dimension habit, Izanami is in control of you, separating you from the sounds that come out of your mouth, even when they follow a priori order. Everything you create is hiluko; your ideas, decisions, desires, etc. and you know they can't be a manifestation of the proper order because Izanami has spoken first. See it for yourselves.

---

* Refer to the KOJIKI, an ancient Japanese text.

KOTOTAMA SOUND EXERCISE

The Kototama sounds in the Amatu Futonorito order.
Read from right to left, vertically and then horizontally,
starting with **A**.

WA	SA	YA	NA	LA	HA	MA	KA	TA	A
WI	SI	YI	NI	LI	HI	MI	KI	TI	I
WE	SE	YE	NE	LE	HE	ME	KE	TE	E
WO	SO	YO	NO	LO	HO	MO	KO	TO	O
WU	SU	YU	NU	LU	HU	MU	KU	TU	U

A (ah) - sounds: the mouth is fully open, big and round.

I (e) - sounds: bite the teeth, opening the lips sideways.

E (a) - sounds: from the I position, open the teeth.

O (o) - sounds: open the mouth half-way, making it round.

U (oo) - sounds: make the mouth small and round.

The KANAGI Order

WA	LA	YA	MA	HA	NA	TA	SA	KA	A
WI	LI	YI	MI	HI	NI	TI	SI	KI	I
WU	LU	YU	MU	HU	NU	TU	SU	KU	U
WE	LE	YE	ME	HE	NE	TE	SE	KE	E
WO	LO	YO	MO	HO	NO	TO	SO	KO	O

The SUGASO Order

WA	NA	LA	MA	YA	HA	SA	KA	TA	A
WO	NO	LO	MO	YO	HO	SO	KO	TO	O
WU	NU	LU	MU	YU	HU	SU	KU	TU	U
WE	NE	LE	ME	YE	HE	SE	KE	TE	E
WI	NI	LI	MI	YI	HI	SI	KI	TI	I

The FUTONOLITO Order

WA	SA	YA	NA	LA	HA	MA	KA	TA	A
WI	SI	YI	NI	LI	HI	MI	KI	TI	I
WE	SE	YE	NE	LE	HE	ME	KE	TE	E
WO	SO	YO	NO	LO	HO	MO	KO	TO	O
WU	SU	YU	NU	LU	HU	MU	KU	TU	U

71

Fear at Midnight

Do you sit at night and early in the morning? Sometimes, when sitting in the forest after midnight you may feel afraid. A strong spirit may come and you'll be so scared that you can't sit there quietly. At that moment, you must decide to die. Fear is only a posteriori life holding on to its existence. If we can return to being the real **A-I**, seeing the source of our consciousness as our own substance, there is nothing there. It is a test to see how far you can reach back to your substance. All fear and suffering is **WA-LE**; it is a difficult exercise.

However much we may understand intellectually, **WA-LE** is a limited world. It is the cause of all our difficulties. When we sit quietly with ourselves, we find we're actually still rooted there and at that time, we can see our terrible fear. This strong spirit I speak of seems worse than any monster and it leaves you feeling helpless. It is your a priori self; your fear means you're still separated from it. We must move one step further to realize I AM and see where it is. We're all stuck in **WA-LE**, Kanagi, but the understanding of **O** dimension is always in Kanagi terms. How far you have moved from there can be seen only at midnight, in how fearful you are of the spirit. There are different a priori energies and therefore, many types of spirits. To experience this means to be seeing from **WA-LE** and it is indeed frightening.

That is why our ancestors practiced sitting from midnight until early in the morning. In Santa Fe, you can do it in the summer; otherwise it is too cold. In Japan, Sakai Sensei and others practiced by staying alone in the mountains. There are many mountain shrines that serve as shelters from the rain. Every year, Sakai Sensei would spend six months in the mountains, meditating and concentrating. As he became old, he reduced this to one or two months. Here, people don't seem to be able to do this kind of serious practice. It is harder to live in Japan economically, but still they go to the mountains to find an inner feeling of certainty; to make sure for themselves.

They study within the symbolic traditions and are given instruction in exactly how to practice, but it is never explained. In symbolic terms, they go to see a particular god or to see what kinds of spirits will appear to them, such as a snake or fox. They are just people who are following their inner desire to see more deeply and some still do it today. They fast, meditate under a waterfall, sleep on a rocky precipice, etc. Their inner feeling gains in sharpness and strength but the meaning of their practice has been lost. As in Aikido, many come to practice but they are not concerned with the final objective of the man who created Aikido. They improve technically, making their bodies stronger and more supple, and they become more sensitive and sharp spiritually, but the final meaning of such exercise is lost. This is a hard way.

Many practicants drop out because they're too tired, having financial difficulties, etc. Perhaps one person will remain out of a hundred who start. It is harder to hold on to one's courage without an answer and the complete satisfaction that comes from having one, but discontinuing practice will not change this. Try to organize a group to do nighttime meditation starting at one a.m. I try to sit when I go overnight fishing, but I haven't done it very much lately. Find a quiet place in the mountains or sit in the dojo. It can be terribly frightening, but it is actually nothing, just things that belong to the a priori world. If you still hold on to a posteriori life, meaning you can't sit quietly when the spirit comes, use the sounds **I E I**. That will help you to see both sides; a priori sees a posteriori and a posteriori sees a priori, moving up and down that way. That is how Izanagi and Izanami exist.

Actually, there are five dimensions of our own manifestation: **A O U E I**. **I** is the center, so it doesn't appear when the energy separates into dimensions. **A O U E** is again divided into yang and yin energies, expanding and concentrating. The Kototama Principle belongs to the action of our own life-will, everything inside of us. What exists outside is secondary. Don't use symbols when you are talking such as heaven, earth, etc. It is all our own matter. The truth is only here.

In the Old Testament, God initiates the first creation; first God and then the creation, thus it has already been separated. Chinese philosophy begins with Tai Chi which then separates into two, Yang and Yin. This is **U-A-WA** (see following diagram). The four dimensions of universal energy are continuously concentrating and become one absolute void, which is **U**. As they are concentrating the energy is still separated but as they come to the end of concentration they become one; meaning nothing. From the end of concentration, this energy starts to turn back towards the expanding direction, and at this moment **U** sound rhythm is born. It is the first manifestation. In Chinese this is symbolized as Tai Chi. In all the various religions it is called the first god. The action for this expansion is the **A** dimension which awakens our consciousness and as this happens we are able to recognize the phenomenal world, **WA**.

There is no separation in the void, therefore individual existences cannot be isolated. It is only during the time of expansion that a posteriori physical life can be recognized through the capacity of **A** dimension Without expansion you can't catch phenomena; nothing can be recognized without **A** lighting up **A-LA**. Recognition means seeing separate, individual existences. If everything is the same and not separated, as in the "black hole", recognition cannot happen. The "black hole" couldn't have even been discovered if not for the fact that we are able to see the other physical existences. Our ability to see different things, to separate the phenomenal world, comes from the capacity of our **E** dimension. **A** is light and **E** is recognition; these dimensions have an expanding direction and are yang. **O** and **U** dimensions have a concentrating activity and therefore are yin. When you give it a name, it is already **WO**.

Tai Chi, the primary **U**, is chaos. There is no

concentration or expansion. Only after the division of **A-WA** can we see what **U** is and only with **E** can we be sure. Nothing can be found in **U** for we can only search with the light of **A**, the expansion of **A-E**. **O** belongs to the activity of **U**. A posteriori **U**, **WU**, is the concentrating energy that holds all physical existence in its space and time. After you make this clear for yourself you will see how concentrating energy does this. It is **U** dimension which creates formed life. For example, H2O, Hydrogen and Oxygen, are atoms that have joined to form water. As life energy concentrates to create the physical world, more atoms join together; the form can't be completed without hydrogen and oxygen. Hydrogen has a nucleus and electrons and within the nucleus itself there is the same order. **U** and **O** have a yin direction; **A** dimension energy is followed by **E**, creating yang activity. **U** is yin and its action creates **O**. **A** separates to **A-WA** and **O** to **O-WO**. One separates to two, then four, eight, etc. **A** expands and **E** follows; **E** never comes first.

A, the light of life, appears at the moment when universal energy is changing from the concentrating direction to expansion. **U** is complete chaos; there is no subject or object, only the sense that something is there. **U** can only be seen with the light of **A** as **WA**. **U** changes to **A**, the subject, which then sees phenomena as **WA**, the object.

This fear at midnight, however brave you think you are, is not a matter of courage. The awakening of the a priori self is really frightening. A priori self is the energy of the total universe. A posteriori **WA**, the physical senses, feels too small and helpless before it. We must put them together and make them the same.

77

When I was a mountain practicant, I was unable to unite them. They should be absolutely one. I didn't have the right teacher to explain this and I didn't know what to do. I can't explain it to you clearly. Fear should not exist in a posteriori life. No one can escape it with the courage from **O** dimension. We must face our own a priori self. One day, as you practice, such a time will come to you. You might become so afraid that you will jump off a cliff in your effort to escape. Remember, use the words **I E I**; draw your sword at least three times, in a loud voice. Awakening from a posteriori self is like emerging from a dream. We must overcome fear by letting the a posteriori self die; bringing a priori and a posteriori together, creating one self. This is the meaning of being re-born.

To See With Light

The sound of **U** is chaos. **A** is the subject, the light of life and **WA** is the object, the phenomenal world seen by the light of **A**. **A** dimension is your inner activity creating the phenomenal world and by its light you see the psychic-spiritual world. Jesus and Buddha exist in **WA**, the phenomena seen from the light of **A**. With this light you realize your own physical existence and you see your body as a vehicle. Finally, it's the sound **A**.

The manifestation of **A** is light; **LA-Y-TE**. Usually, we understand **A** in a separated way, believing we are here and grasping the phenomenal world there. To separate is to continue seeing the world from a relative point of view. With the realization of the fifty sounds, we can say, "I see myself and recognize it as a phenomenon." Without this realization, you won't understand, you'll circle around in the hell-world created by your intelligence, blaming others for your misery and never able to save yourself.

With our purification, we can clarify who is I AM. If we

do not know what it is to be a human being it is useless. Everyone uses the words "I know" without specifying who is I AM. The implication is that, "I know more than you do, and therefore don't need to study with you because I already have it." This reflects our belief and our civilization continues to be carried on in this ridiculous way. What you have is the property of your memory, which means intelligence. The ability to store things in the mind is only a part of human capacity.

What kinds of things are kept in the mind? You think you are what you remember and say, "I know," but you aren't certain whether what's in your memory is true or not. You never actually studied it first hand, you just recorded it from somewhere. Someone says for example, "I am a Christian and believe in the existence of Jesus. I saw him and he spoke to me." Are you sure? You haven't investigated it to see if it's true. With the capacity of **A** dimension, the psychic world is seen as phenomena. You hear voices, see angels, or picture the form of a man or woman and you know who they are from descriptions you've read or portraits you've seen. When you meditate and a vision appears to you, it assumes a form you can recognize from past knowledge. Upon having this kind of experience someone will say, "Jesus spoke to me directly because I am so pure." A Buddhist, seeing the same vision, would call it Buddha and feel the same strengthening in his belief; "I'm sure God exists," or Jesus or Buddha. Are these interpretations true or not? You realize these visions based on what you have learned, to which you add a little imagination. Actually, there's no name at all, it was added after the experience! With this type of mistaken viewpoint you will lose your way and never come to the final truth, symbolized as the Blue Bird country or Garden of Eden. You will be shut out forever because the guardian angel will not let you step inside. The Garden of Eden is our pure birthplace and the source of human capacity. If we can't be there, what is there to talk about? You believe this borrowed knowledge to be yourself but it is only imitation.

In the story of "The Emperor's Nightingale", the gaudy mechanical bird was the delight of his court, but when the emperor was dying it was only the song of the real bird that could restore him to life.

Our ancestors left us the way to return to our source. With the Kototama Principle, we can find out very clearly who is I AM, how human capacity manifests physically and spiritually, and in what order. It may have taken many millions of years to complete and perfect the final life principle which is the fifty sounds. It was then hidden in order to guide humanity towards perfection of the material-scientific civilization. For the last eight thousand years, all of our energy has been directed towards that goal. The task has not yet been completed for we have only just arrived at the level of the atomic world. We still ride in uncomfortable cars, needing to watch the road and even still having accidents. Our scientific civilization is far from perfect. We are not yet able to freely use total universal energy in our daily lives. When this civilization is complete we'll discover how to build flying saucers. Our cars will automatically avoid accidents. We will drive along airways, not bothering with roads, flying freely with the automatic synchronization between energies. We are very proud of our present day accomplishments, but upon serious reflection, they are not so impressive.

We will move into the space of the universe as our phenomenal world, using its energy. The Kototama Principle shows us that all phenomena is the same as the self; I am the universe. Our ancestors grasped this and clarified it with sound. It's impossible to understand as long as you hang on to your intellectual knowledge. There is no scientific proof of the existence of the fifty life rhythms. With the scientific approach we aren't able to acquire such knowledge. What doesn't fit into the scientific world doesn't exist and that's a very small world indeed. Our knowledge is based only on physical existence so you can't see the creator, controller of the life rhythms and the pure self. Standing on the physical, we can only see a posteriori existence. We can not find the pure self going from **WA** to **A**. Our body is just a physical constitution. Its source is the light of life, the life-will and life-power which create our body and give it all of its capacities. This is the action of **I** dimension.

If you look into a strong light, you cannot see behind it, but from the perspective of the light, it can see you. Everyone, as they search, should light up themselves as pure total human beings in order to see clearly. You cannot see from the phenomenal side, the light blinds you from there. You can't see behind the sunrise but from the sun you can see all the phenomena of earth. What I'm asking you to do is a very hard exercise. The viewpoint from the Kototama Principle is exactly opposite from that of science. Using that of science you can't see anything and therefore it only confuses you. To see how you make your own light, you're obliged to practice putting your sounds in order. You must open your **A** dimension, the spiritual light that comes through your physical being. It will change your viewpoint. Yesterday all you saw was the limited world with your physical senses, but once you've opened your life's light and see from there, everything is different. If you try to tell other people about it, those who aren't open won't understand you and will say you're crazy. They can not imagine what you've seen or understand what you know. The way you speak will be outside the realm of their experience and it won't make any sense to them. I see this and feel pity because they haven't experienced it, but once you've opened your inner light there is no desire to argue. It doesn't matter. They are free to speak and I am here.

It's as if knowing arithmetic; 1+1, 1-2, etc. and thinking that it represents the complete theory of mathematics. When someone introduces the concepts of higher math, the person can't believe in their existence. He has no other knowledge and can't conceive that anything else is possible. Everyone has different levels of mental development. It becomes a big argument in this society; those with elementary minds thinking they know the truth. What do you do? You can't ask them to step back, so you just stay away. You can see their mistake, but can't force what you know on them. They can't judge you because they do not see what you have inside. If you have a strong love and desire for the oneness of the human family, you may try to make them understand in order to free them. You may feel that this is your mission, but they will see that love as an act of violence. Your desire is to give them your purest, highest love but they will not receive it that way, so there's nothing more to do.

That's why it isn't allowed to speak of the Kototama Principle with the idea of forcing an understanding. If someone is truly searching and they seek you out one day saying they feel something is missing, only then can you help with all your love. If you're not asked, don't try. No matter how rich or famous or intelligent a person may be, you'd just be wasting your time and energy. Only in asking will they be given; they must knock at the door for it to open.

People today aren't searching, they're only curious about a new idea. They prefer to share with you what they know, to show how clever they are and to compete with you. You needn't give them your energy. An appetite already satiated must refuse more food no matter how much finer it may be for there is no space left. Just show them respect for their intelligence and let them know you think they're much greater than you are, since they're so anxious to show their superiority. Listen and when they make you tired, excuse yourself. Never use power or violence; don't make that mistake!

The Meaning
of the Word

Today, April 23rd, is the most important Jizo Bosatsu ceremony of the year. Our ancestors are all happy that we are here. We could not exist, physically or spiritually, without the roots from which we've sprung; we cannot ignore our physical and spiritual beginnings. Our spiritual ancestors, although not of the physical world, nevertheless materialize in the human body. All material existence was created first in a priori, from the void. This means our physical ancestors passed through the void a million years ago, just as we have today. In the absolute void, there is no time or space. When you step back far enough into yourself, you will come to the void, having no beginning or end. It is the center of the universe and the self manifests from there to here-now. Theoretical science recognizes the void as the "center" of the physical universe, yet it is also the source of our being. If we can recognize who is I AM, we will see our own creation, second by second, manifesting from there to here-now.

85

This happens instantaneously; there is no time or space. We emerge in the order of the rhythms of the fifty Kototama sounds that manifest each second to here. We must always hold on to self as the source; we came from there and manifest here.

For thousands of years, this study has been lost to us, the ability to see our self. There is no one who can say what a human being is without resorting to the use of symbols. A thousand times a day we say, I AM, I know, I do, I go, but the question is how? We have only an intellectual understanding of I, which doesn't answer anything. Out of our blindness, we lie to ourselves. To understand on an intellectual level is always a lie. This is what creates this civilization and its inherent confusion. If you use the words "I go", everyone "knows" it means to move forward. Actually, the word "go" is the combination of two sounds; **KO-O**. The meaning of **KO**, in the fifty sounds, is to step back, move behind and pass through from here-now, manifesting in a backwards direction. It does not mean forward movement. When you vocalize the sounds in the word go, your inner life rhythm says one thing and your body does something else, going completely against your self. The word is a god; when our physical actions go against our god, how are we to save ourselves? We are always separated from the sounds we make and the actions of our body. That which follows intellectual knowledge is always in opposition to the action and desire of our pure self.

We've forgotten how to awaken our real capacity as human beings. We put our trust in our capacity as a computer to receive and store more information based on our physical sense experiences and those things we've learned from others. No one asks what is behind these facts, our only interest is to put them in storage. We never question if the perception is correct or not. It seems too impractical and it won't get us anywhere. We don't try to judge or examine first; we simply accept it. When Einstein became an authority, we stopped examining or judging what he said, just accepting it like the word of god. Similarly, whatever was spoken by Jesus or Buddha has been memorized as the truth, and any contradictory ideas are automatically incorrect. Anyone with a different understanding opposes the truth, particularly when it is held to be sacred, and therefore it isn't possible to make agreements amongst ourselves. No matter what pure theory is presented, if it doesn't fit what you already understand, either it is completely unacceptable or it is received with an underlying ambiguity. There can never be any real understanding between human beings with this kind of imitation knowledge.

We identify with acquired knowledge as being ourselves and anything other than that feels like an attack on our cherished beliefs. We might be undone! If it were the truth instead of a symbol, and we were purely responding to it, everyone would feel the same and there would be no argument.

Today's knowledge is a delusion because it is based on imitation. No matter how much talk there is of making a peaceful world, our actions always take the other direction. There are so many people who hope and work hard to bring it about, but they can't. We're always doing the opposite thing, meanwhile cheating ourselves and going against our creator.

First we must awaken our original capacity as human beings. We must stay in our inner self because our heads are asleep and cannot see the life inside. Holding on to our psychic life means allowing our own substance, the essence of our being, to act through this body. We do not do this however. We turn off our consciousness and block its flow, hence rejecting our own manifestation and our capacity cannot realize itself.

So that we may reawaken, we must participate in this Jizo Bosatsu ceremony, through prayer and meditation before our ancestors. We must keep a meek mind and ask forgiveness for getting "stuck" and losing our way. We should sincerely express gratitude to our ancestors for trying to help us find the way of truth. We carry them with us but can't hear their voice. We don't listen and then we fall into error. We must apologize and ask forgiveness for our stupidity and thank them for their divine love and continued protection. We are never abandoned by them nor do they cease from trying to guide us on the path. At least once a month we must say these things with all sincerity. There is no excuse not to attend this ceremony once a month. Jizo Bosastsu exists inside of you and you owe it to yourself. There is no escape from your own substance. Unfortunately, people don't realize this and wish to be free of such obligations. Without realizing what it is to be a human being, they just move aimlessly about in this world, unaware of their own humanity. I can guarantee that they will never arrive at anything that is truly meaningful.

Once a month, let's participate in this small ceremony together so we don't forget the debt we owe our ancestors. Why not?

About Freedom and Discipline

by Katsuharu K. Nakazono

To The Practicants:

In the past few months, I have seen a few students interrupt their classes or drop out. This is a mistake. So, to avoid having others make the same mistake, I am writing this article.

For Aikido, medicine or any other study where there is a Tao, the senseis have had to follow a discipline, one which must be followed very strictly if it is to be the practice of a real human being. That is why it hasn't changed for thousands of years, nor is there anything that can be changed. Our present system of education emphasizes freedom, without knowing the meaning of the word. Everyone talks about it with their mouths. When someone is told he's made a mistake, he feels, "I am free, so please don't bother me with criticism." That person doesn't reflect about himself and never tries to improve; he's always looking for an easy way to live. That is society's present understanding of life, but we have to think further about freedom and liberty. What is it? In my opinion, liberty means never being caught, physically or spiritually, by any situation or object. If you are required to do something, but you don't want to, and you don't, is that freedom? To achieve real freedom, we need to practice being human, and this, of necessity, has a strict discipline.

If someone resents that discipline and sees it as a means of control, to make him a slave, I can't even begin to talk to him. For example, to be called a sensei requires at least ten years of study with a demonstrated ability in that study, so naturally that person would have the experience it takes to be a sensei. In Aikido, each sensei has a different teaching method, with a different understanding of the forms, such as Shihonage, etc. However, in the world of Aikido, the meaning of Shihonage never changes. If, after a few years or even a few months of study under a sensei, someone tries to teach others (such people do exist), he is rationalizing that it would be unkind of him not to. Someone would ask to do Shihonage with him, a movement he knows, and he thinks that if he doesn't show him how, it just wouldn't be right. Or else, he may be aware of his lack of capacity but teaches anyway, for money or false honor. This type of person, whom I call an impostor, usually has many students because he has no love, doesn't know the truth and, consequently, is never hard on them. He doesn't need to be nor can he be; he lets them do as they please and, of course, they feel most agreeable towards him. This may be good for business, but I must say to anyone who conducts their activities from the heart and with a genuine desire to help others, a business based on a lie cannot last. It will end quickly because not many people are stupid enough to continue paying a high price for junk.

To return to the point, any sensei will ask a student with good capacity or a desire to learn, to practice with a strict discipline. The sensei himself has already done it, could not have skipped over it and still walks that road because without that particular discipline you can't walk that way. Even so, some people misunderstand and think that whatever the sensei asks them to do, out of his love and intent to further their development, is coming from his desire to control, making them his slaves. They can't stand it and they slip away. It is really pitiful because they are so sure they're right, but I can't stop them. If someone in your family, for example, in his ignorance were going to eat poisonous mushrooms and you knew that they were, with your love for him do you think you could just stand there and watch him eat them? I'm sure you would try to stop him, perhaps by first talking to him. If he still didn't understand, you might hit him and, finally, you might just grab the mushrooms and throw them out, putting your life there to help him. If he were yearning for those mushrooms, when you took them away he would feel you'd been very hard and he'd feel dissatisfied. If he could reflect at all, he might look it up in a book or ask a mushroom specialist, or even easier, listen to your advice. In that case, there would be no need for him to die. There are some who would think that you stopped them out of love but that you didn't really know what you were talking about. They don't trust you and begin to hold a grudge against you. They'll eat the mushrooms when you're not looking and die. It's pitiful, but they got what they wanted and you were not there to help them. Discipline is like that.

That's why any sensei is very strict, especially with serious students. As you make progress, the way becomes more strict. One day, you understand why, and, at that time, your sensei gives you permission to teach other people and your capacity is such that others call you sensei. If you stop your practice at that point, it is not good enough. When your sensei gives you the authority to teach, it only means you can see what is good and bad and can keep yourself on the right path, guiding others the same way. You cannot, however, say you're free. Freedom is physical and spiritual; it means whatever you think or like, however you move or talk, is in perfect harmony with the total universe. The total universe is yourself, in Heaven and earth; I am only one. I am all there is and that place is called free. The Kototama Principle calls it Naka-Ima. You will not attain Naka-Ima by dancing Aikido, sleeping Zen, doing marijuana, Yoga meditation, dreaming philosophy, etc. You have to be very strict with yourself, taking one step at a time, and continuing to practice. At that time, your sensei will be very strict with you, and you, yourself, must strictly observe the discipline and continue practicing, otherwise you'll never reach Naka-Ima. If you don't like it, if it just seems too stupid to you, stop immediately and step away from the whole truth, because you'll be wasting your very, very important time and will just be disappointed.

ABOUT THE AUTHOR

Hinomoto Masahilo no Mikoto Nakazono

O Sensei Nakazono devoted his entire life's energy pursuing the way to the final truth. This quest took him to near perfection of the traditional martial arts; years of rigorous spiritual practices; and decades of testing, questioning and perfecting all aspects of traditional oriental therapies. It led him to Ueshiba Sensei and mastery of Aikido; to Professor Ohsawa and the practice of Macrobiotics; to Sakai Sensei, the master of healing with the hands; and to Ogasawara Sensei, who guided him toward understanding the Kototama Principle.

This lifetime pursuit to grasp a unified understanding of the Universe has resulted in a practical basis of health care.

Born in Kagoshima District, southern Japan, in 1918, Sensei Nakazono's earliest experiences of healing came from his mother, a nurse-midwife who used foods, herbs, poultices and massage in her work. She was highly respected and widely recognized for her ability to turn breech babies and demand for her services continued throughout his childhood.

His study of Kendo began at age six. When Sensei Nakazono retired, he held the rank of 7th Dan. Before his teens, Sensei began concentrating on the practice of Judo and began intensive professional studies when he was 14. By 1933, he earned his Black Belt in Judo and a year later began a two year apprenticeship in the study and practice of Acupuncture with Dr. Juzo Motoyama in Nagasaki. In 1938, he received his license as a "Bone-Setter," an osteopathic specialty in structural repair and manipulation available only to 3rd Dan Judo instructors who had undergone specific rigorous training.

He was trained in Aikido, a martial art for self-purification, by its founder, Ueshiba Sensei. During the 1960s, he was the World Aikido Federation representative to Europe and North Africa and Director of the European Aikido Federation. He retired with the rank of 9th Dan.

It was Ueshiba Sensei who introduced him to the Kototama Principle, saying it was the foundation of the principles of Aikido. However, Ueshiba Sensei continued to use the traditional metaphors and symbols by way of explanation and his teaching of the Unified World appeared theoretical or metaphysical. There were to be 18 more years of searching before Sensei Nakazono would come in contact with Ogasawara Sensei.

A professor named George Ohsawa developed some interesting nutritional ideas which he termed "Macrobiotics." Sensei Nakazono's association with Professor Ohsawa began in 1950 and their close relationship lasted over ten years. In 1955, Sensei left Japan and traveled to India where he established the

Universal Institute. There he treated mental and physical disorders using Ohsawa's system; i.e., he diagnosed according to Macrobiotic theory and personally prepared each of his patient's meals. He treated there in this manner for three years. Upon his return to Japan, he was introduced to the renowned master of handwork therapy, Sakai Sensei. Master Sakai taught Sensei his own method: Te A Te (Spiritual Hand Treatment) and continued to guide him until his death. It was Master Sakai who fully grasped the spirit of finite form-Jizo Bosatsu. This "treatment by spirit" led Sakai Sensei to unique diagnostic powers and treatment methods which he passed on to Sensei Nakazono.

The first Aikido dojo outside of Japan was founded by Sensei in 1958, in Singapore. In 1960, he was a martial arts consultant to the government of South Vietnam.

In France, where he settled with his family in the early 1960s, he established the Kan Nagara Institute and began training European students in Aikido and therapy techniques. He traveled throughout Europe and North Africa during his 11 years in France. When he departed for the United States in 1972, he had over 40,000 European Aikido students and student practitioners of Natural Therapy.

The study of the Kototama Principle began when he established contact with Ogasawara Sensei. Though his teacher was in Japan and he was in France, the effect of his studies and the correspondences between teacher and student transformed his life - thoughts, speech, Aikido, therapy work - all dimensions underwent profound transformation. Kototama meditation became Kototama life. The movements of Aikido changed, viewpoints changed, the understanding of Natural Therapy changed and its application took on an entirely new meaning.

A six month visit to the U.S. in 1970 resulted in his decision to establish a center of learning in Santa Fe, New Mexico. In 1972, he arrived in Santa Fe, opened a medical clinic and dojo and began teaching Aikido and Oriental Medicine as manifestations of the Kototama Principle.

Weekly discourses on the Kototama Principle began and publishing efforts were initiated; students increased and the load at his clinic grew. In January 1973, patients of Sensei introduced an Acupuncture Practice Act in the State Senate. This was the first acupuncture legislation ever considered in the United States.

His healing capacities became widely known and it was necessary for him to ask his son, Katsuharu K. Nakazono Sensei, to come to Santa Fe and assist him. His son, also a highly ranked Aikido master and Acupuncturist, arrived in Santa Fe in 1974. By 1977, he and his son had treated well over 4,000 patients who came from all parts of the country and various parts of the world seeking his unique methods of treatment. His patient waiting list grew, people were waiting two months to be seen and it was decided to teach Kototama Life Medicine on a formal basis. In the fall of 1978, he enrolled his first class at the Kototama Institute.

The Kototama Institute provided a formal education in the basics of traditional Acupuncture, a post-graduate clinical program in Kototama Life Medicine and a ten year doctoral program for those seeking to be Doctors of Kototama Life Medicine.

Sensei Nakazono was a consultant to the Hawaiian Acupuncture Board, and was widely read in Japanese professional journals. In the spring of 1985, returned to France at the invitation of the French Osteopathic Association and the French Aikido Federation as a guest lecturer.

In 1984, Santa Fe citizens bestowed on him the award, "Living Treasure of Santa Fe." During the 1985 Legislative session, the New Mexico State Senate honored Sensei Nakazono with the Award of Exceptional Achievement "for having inspired and directed the passage of the New Mexico Acupuncture Act, for having established schools and for the professional practice and recognition of acupuncture in this State since 1972."

Through his classes, his patients and his writings, Sensei Nakazono has asked the world to seriously study the Kototama Principle. It is for all humanity. This is the message of his life's work.

Other Books By Mikoto Masahilo Nakazono

INOCHI - The Book of Life   1984

The Source of the Present Civilization   1990

The Real Sense of Natural Therapy   1992

Soon to be available:
The Source of the Old and New Testaments   1990

Please direct correspondence to :
                    www.kototamabooks.com
                              or
                    Kototama Books
                    2526 Camino San Patricio
                    Santa Fe, New Mexico 87505
                    505-471-5194

For editions in French and Spanish, please contact:
                    J. Akehiko Tavernier
                    Moulin De Choisy
                    77320 SAINT REMY De La VANNE
                    FRANCE
                    TEL: 011-33-1-64-04-0480
                    FAX: 011-33-1-64-20-2420